Couleur Me a Cupcake
Livres de coloriage pour enfants

Coloring Pages for Kids

Coloring Pages for Kids
An imprint of Ciparum LLC

Couleur Me a Cupcake Livres de coloriage pour enfants
© 2017 Ciparum LLC
All rights reserved.
ISBN-10:1-63589-325-9
ISBN-13:978-1-63589-325-0

Coloring Pages for Kids

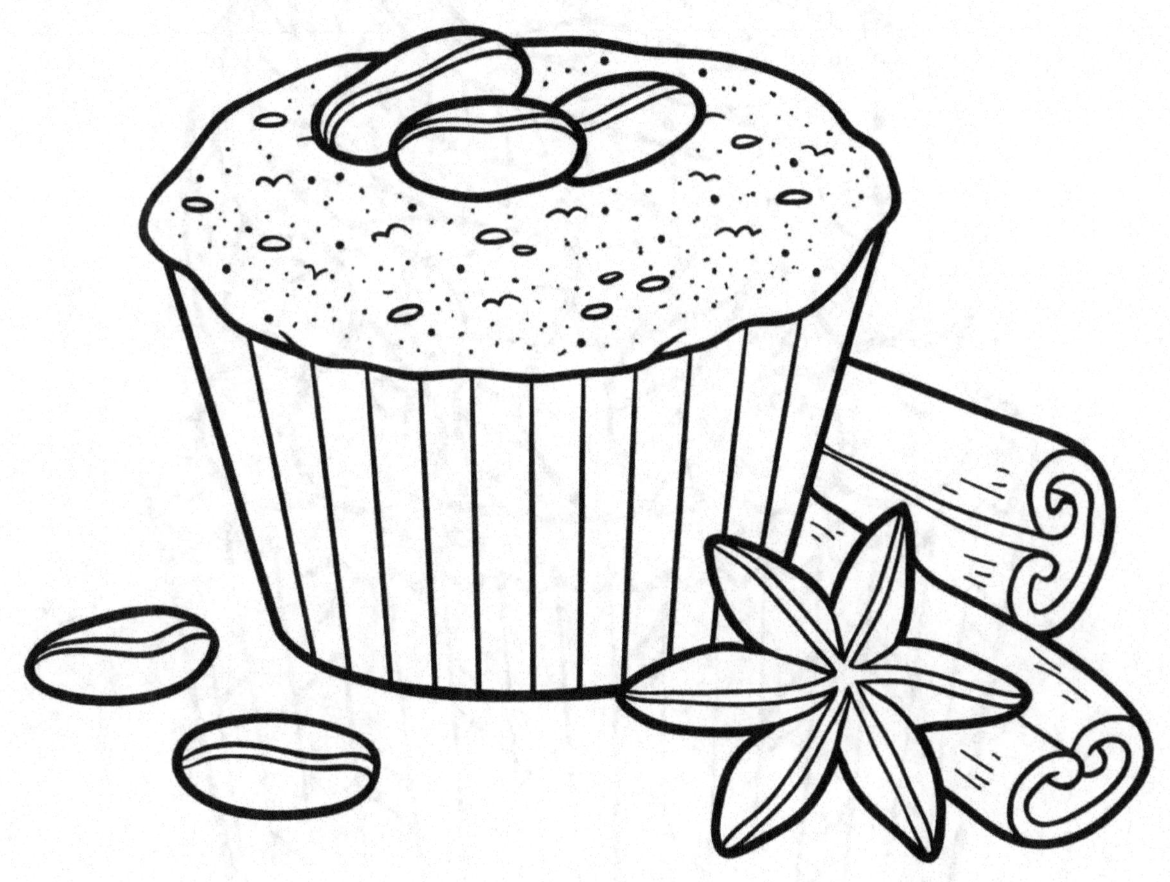

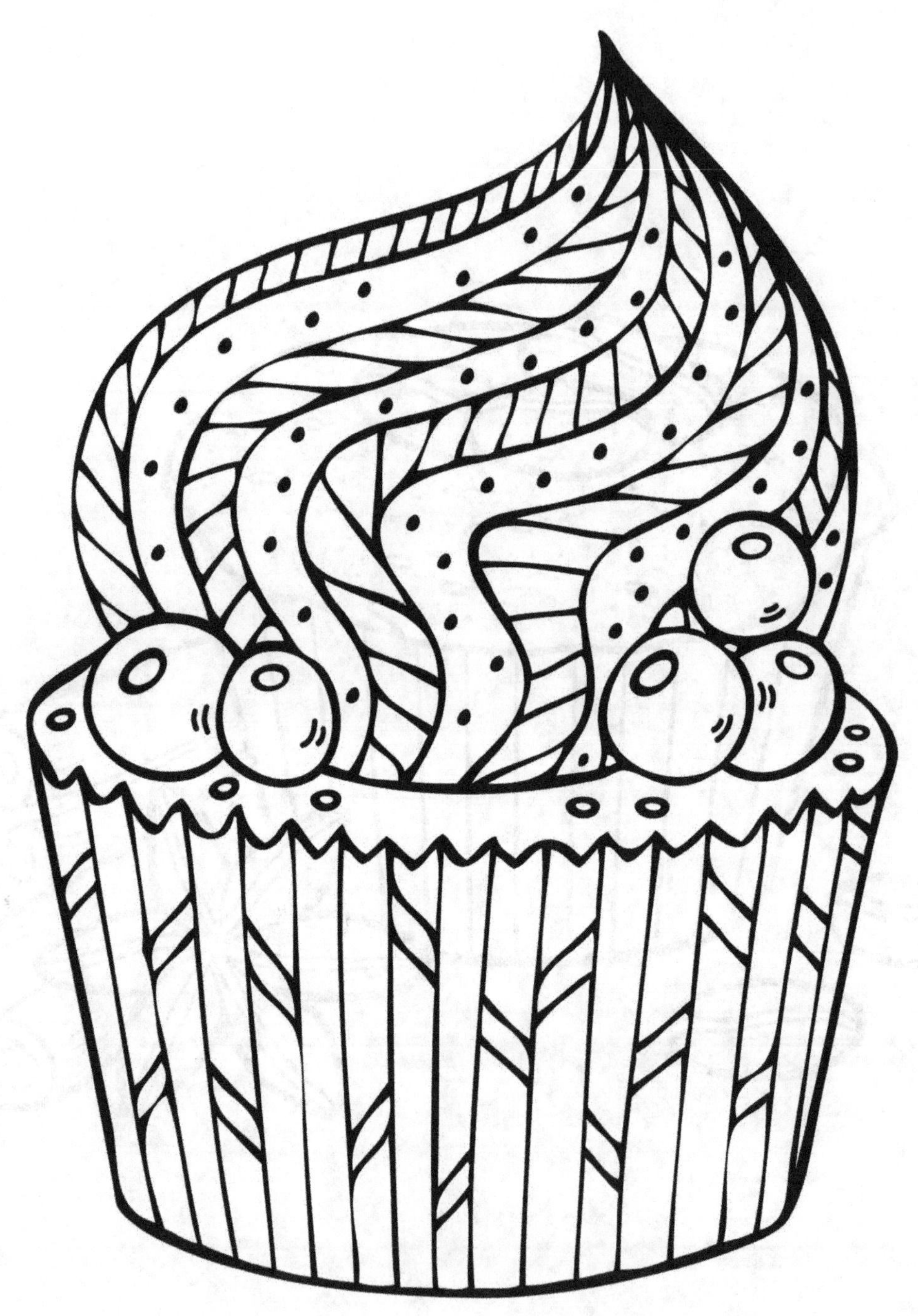

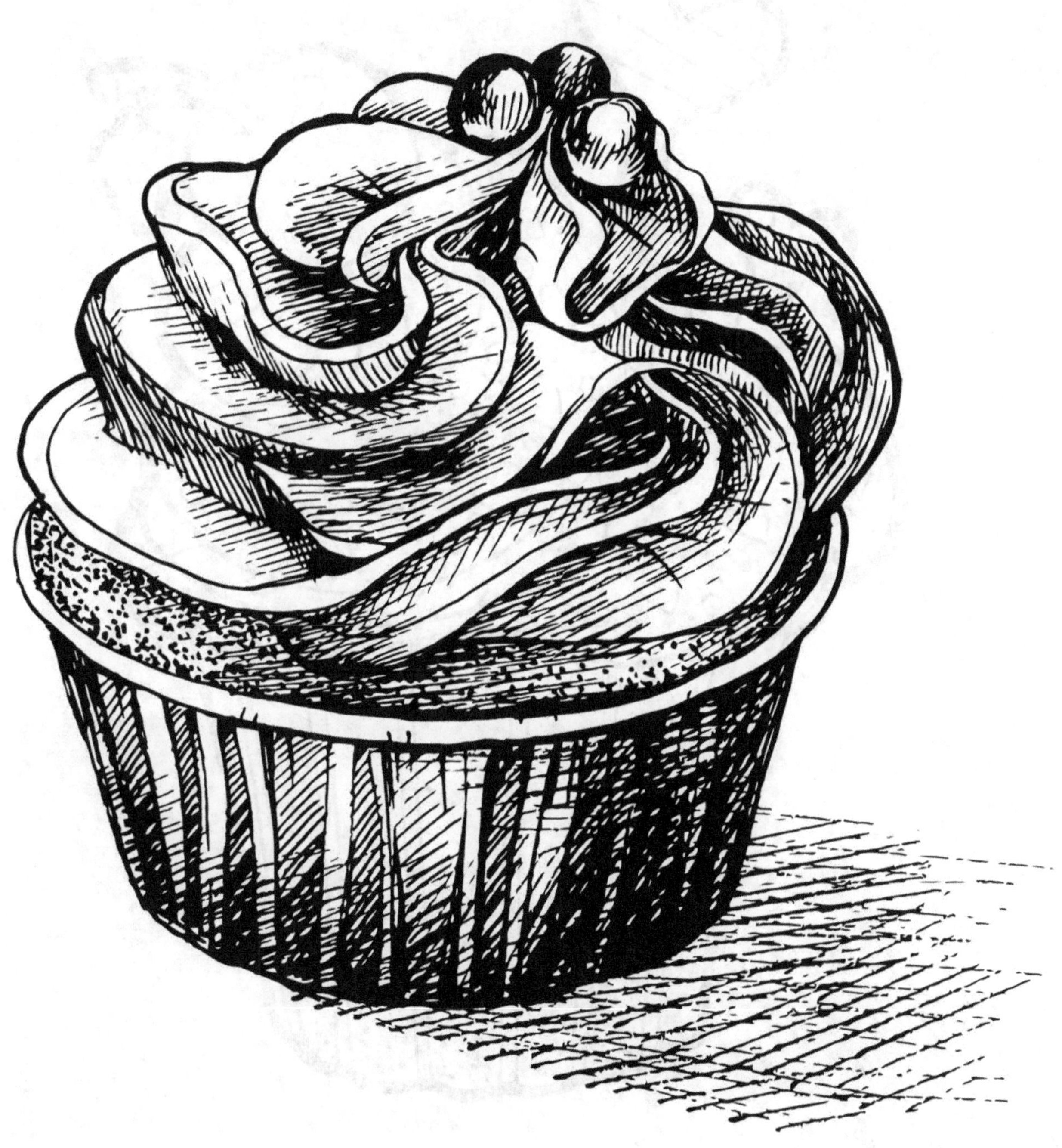

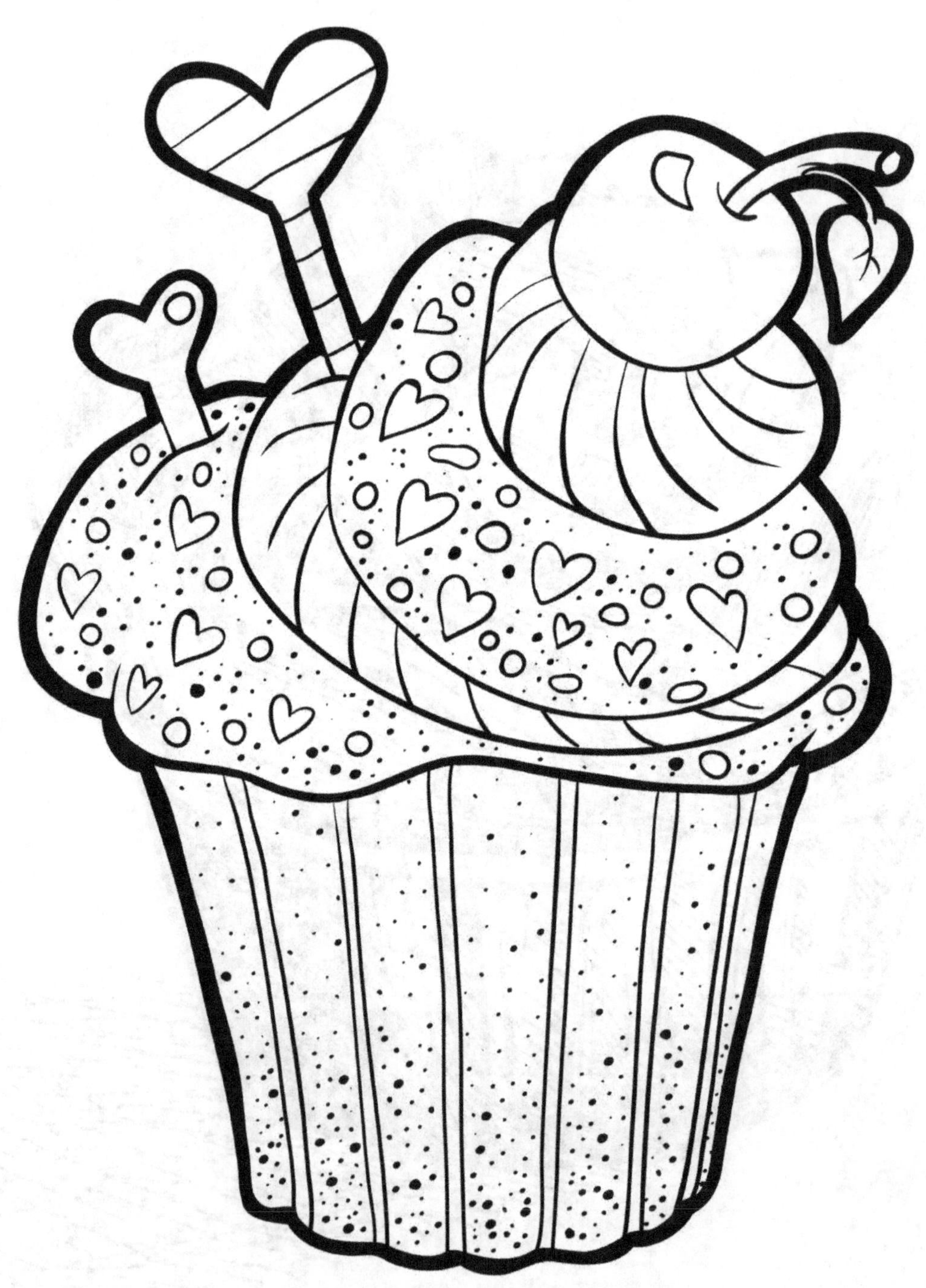

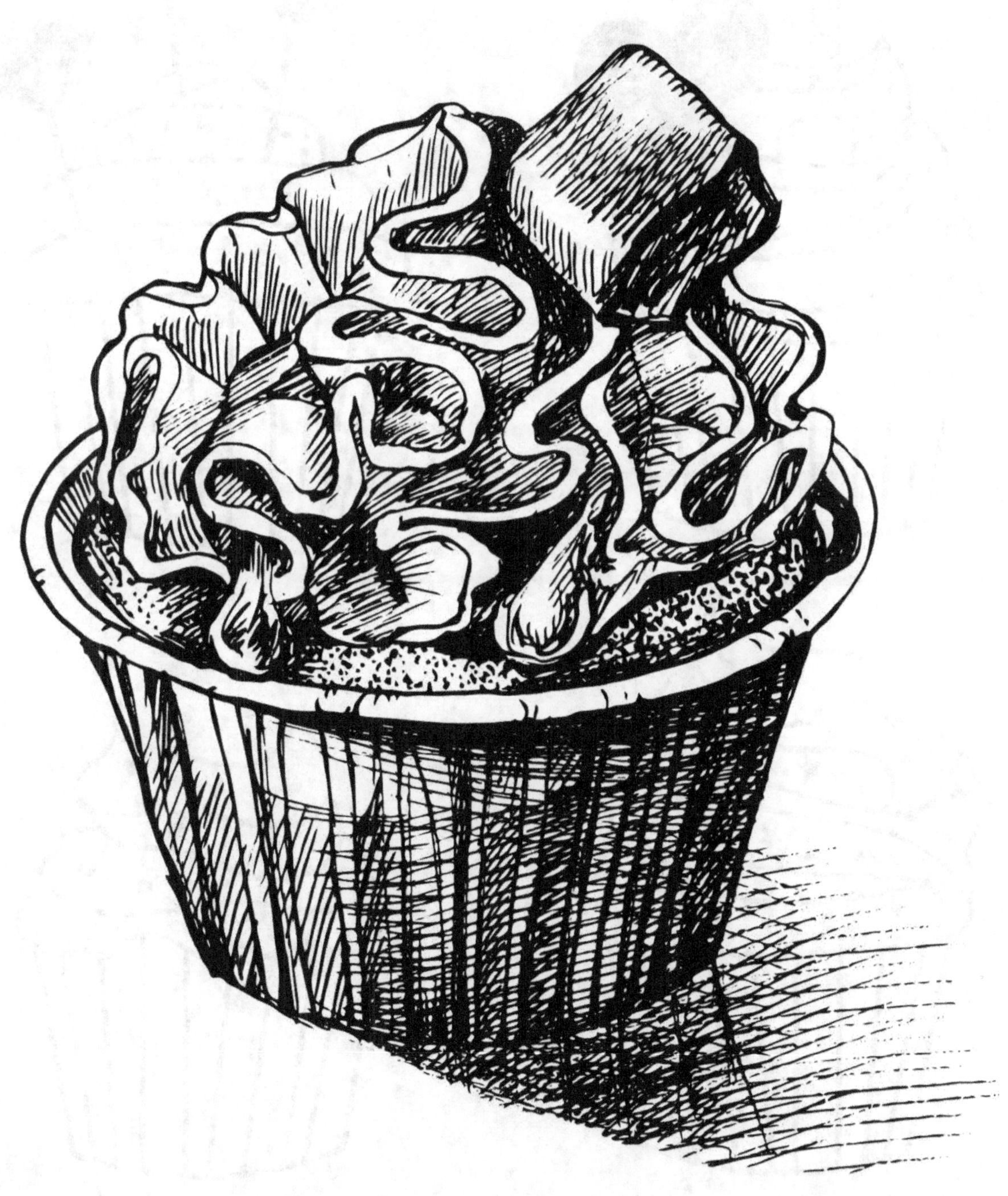

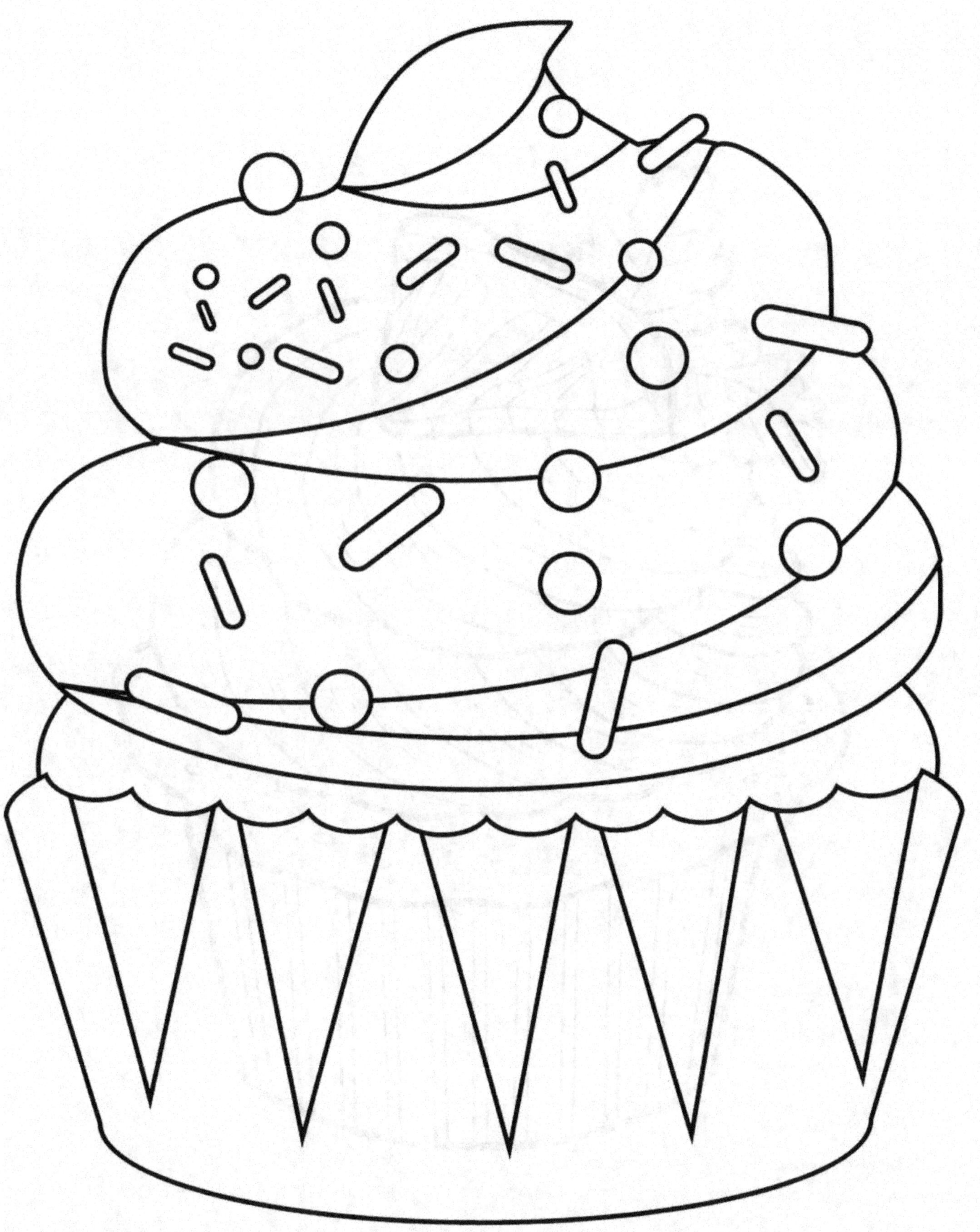

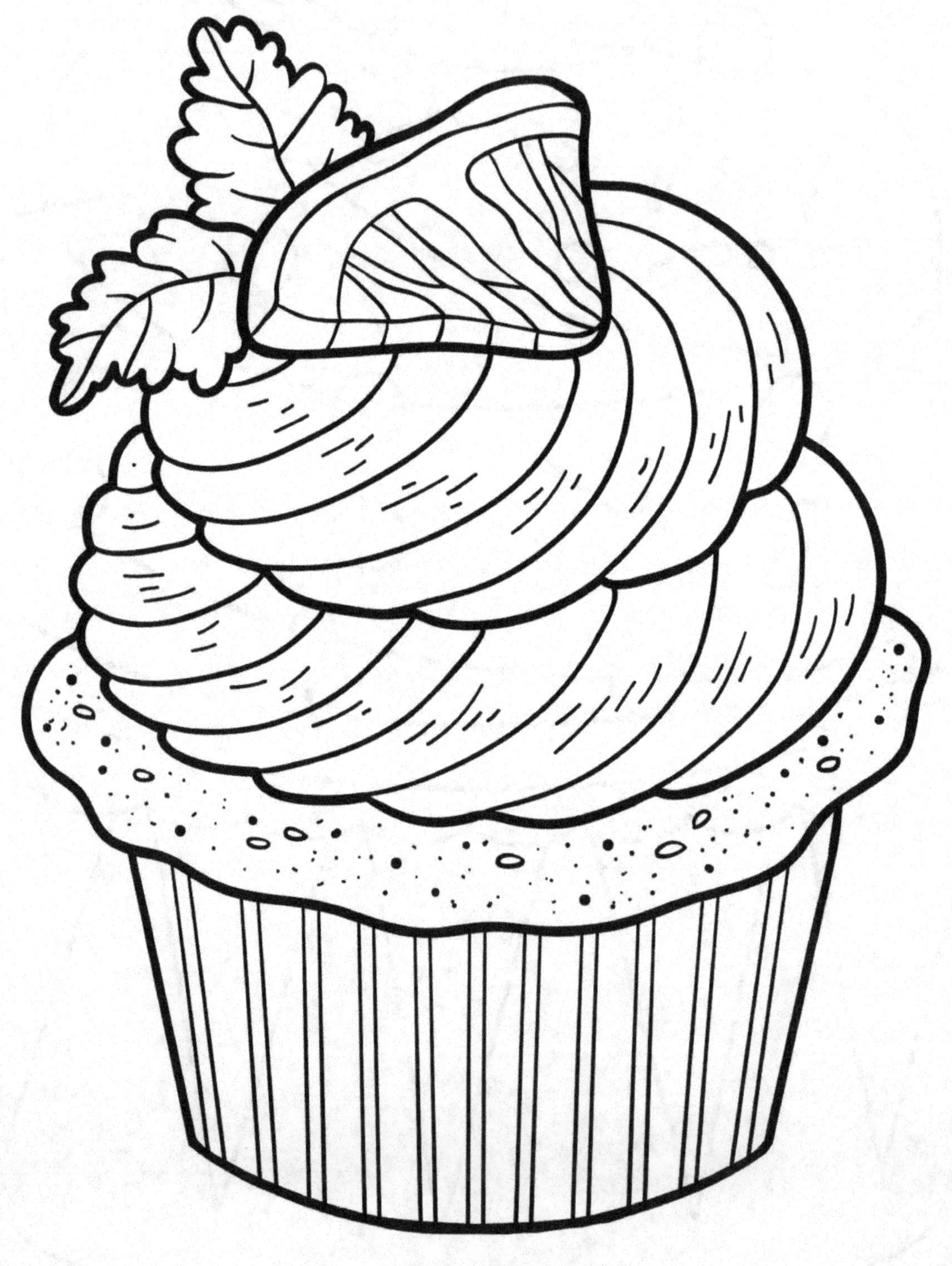

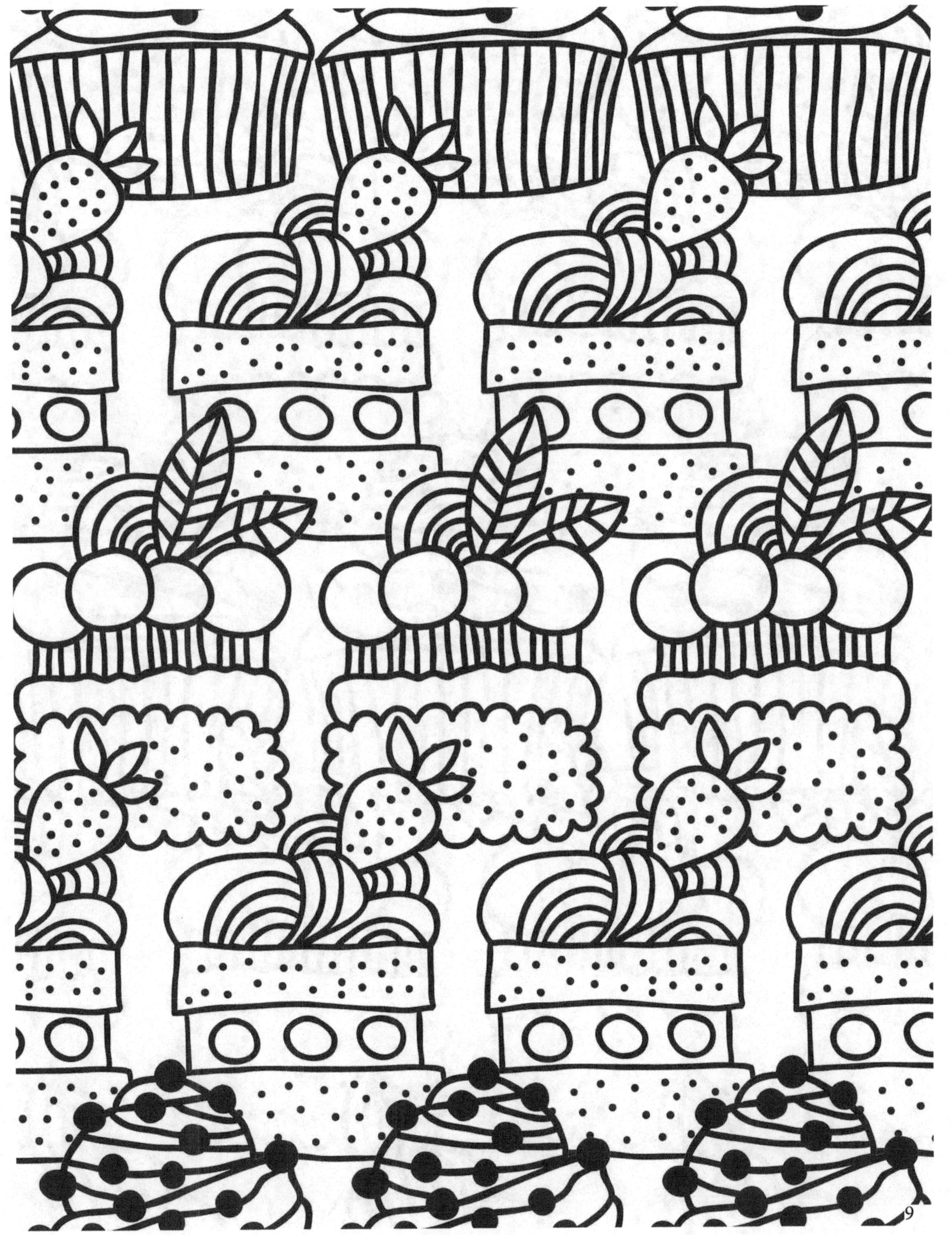

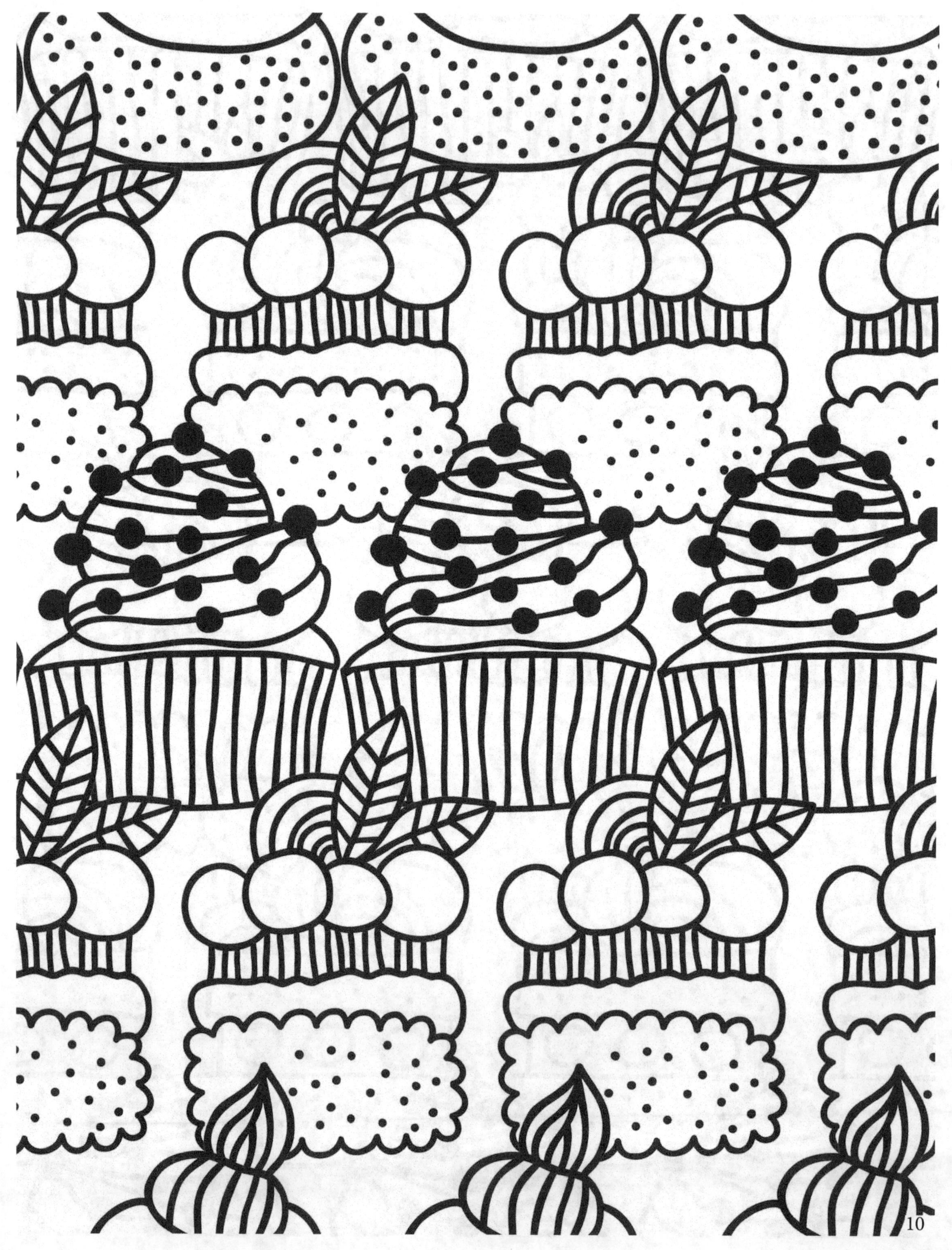

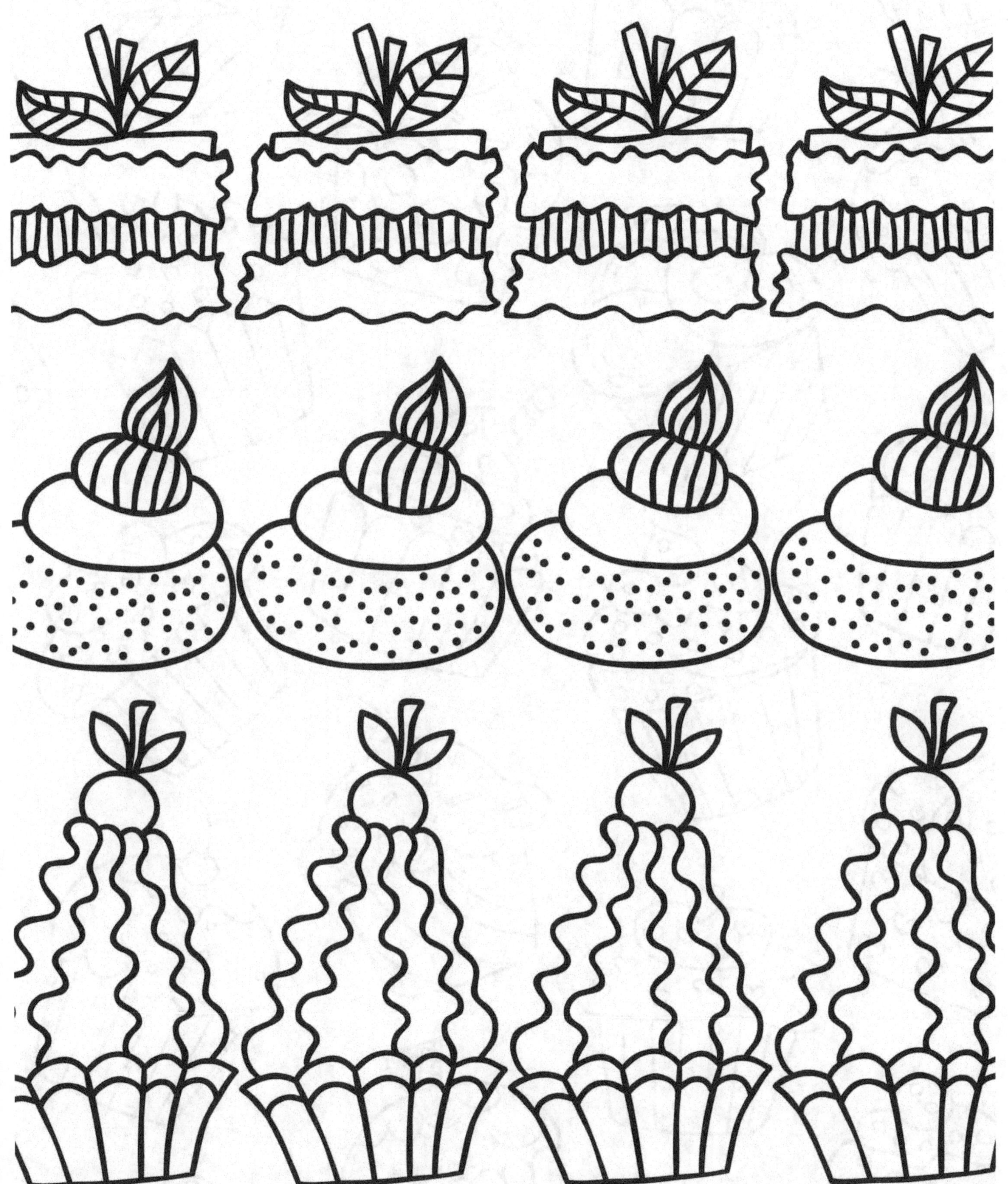

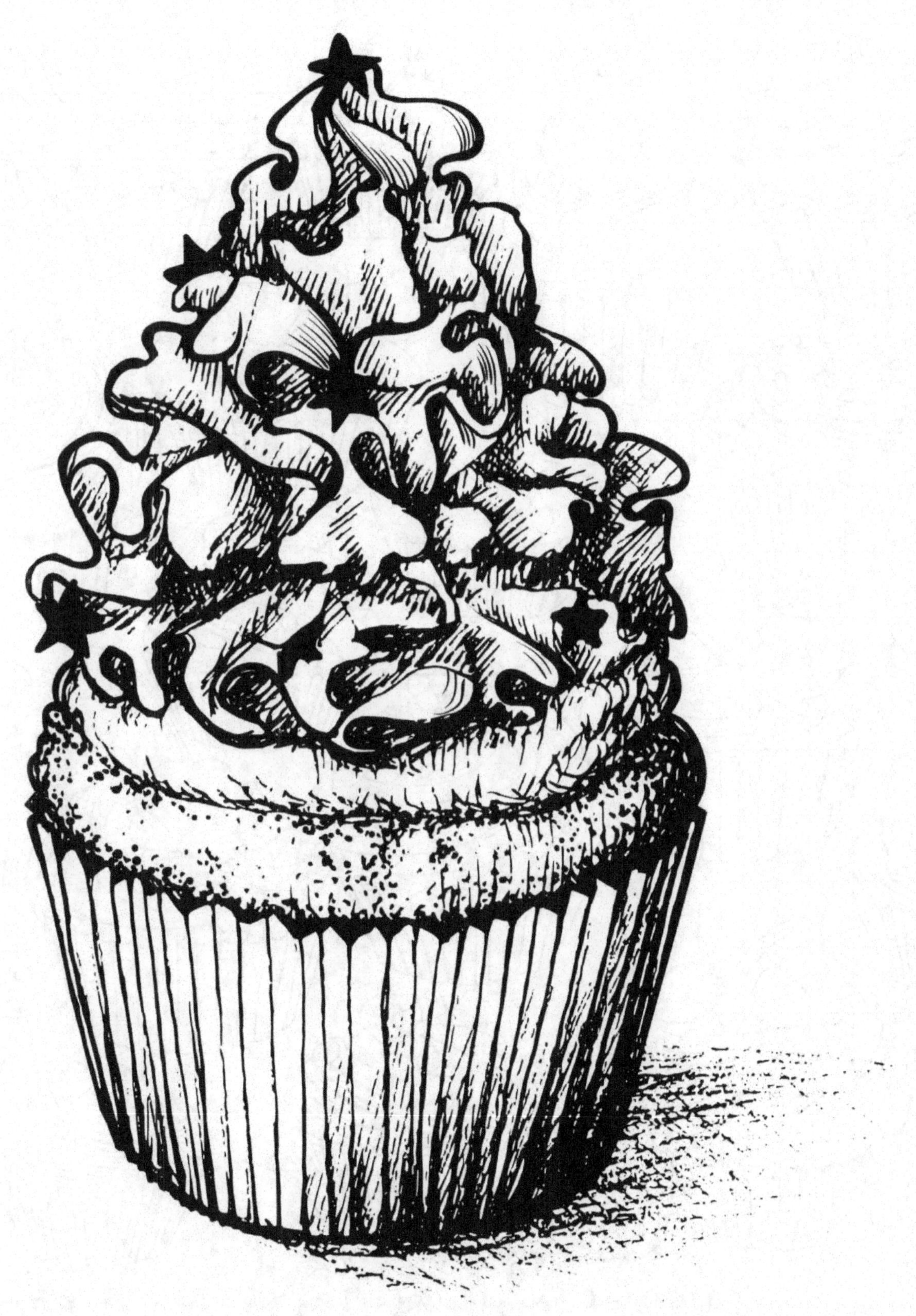

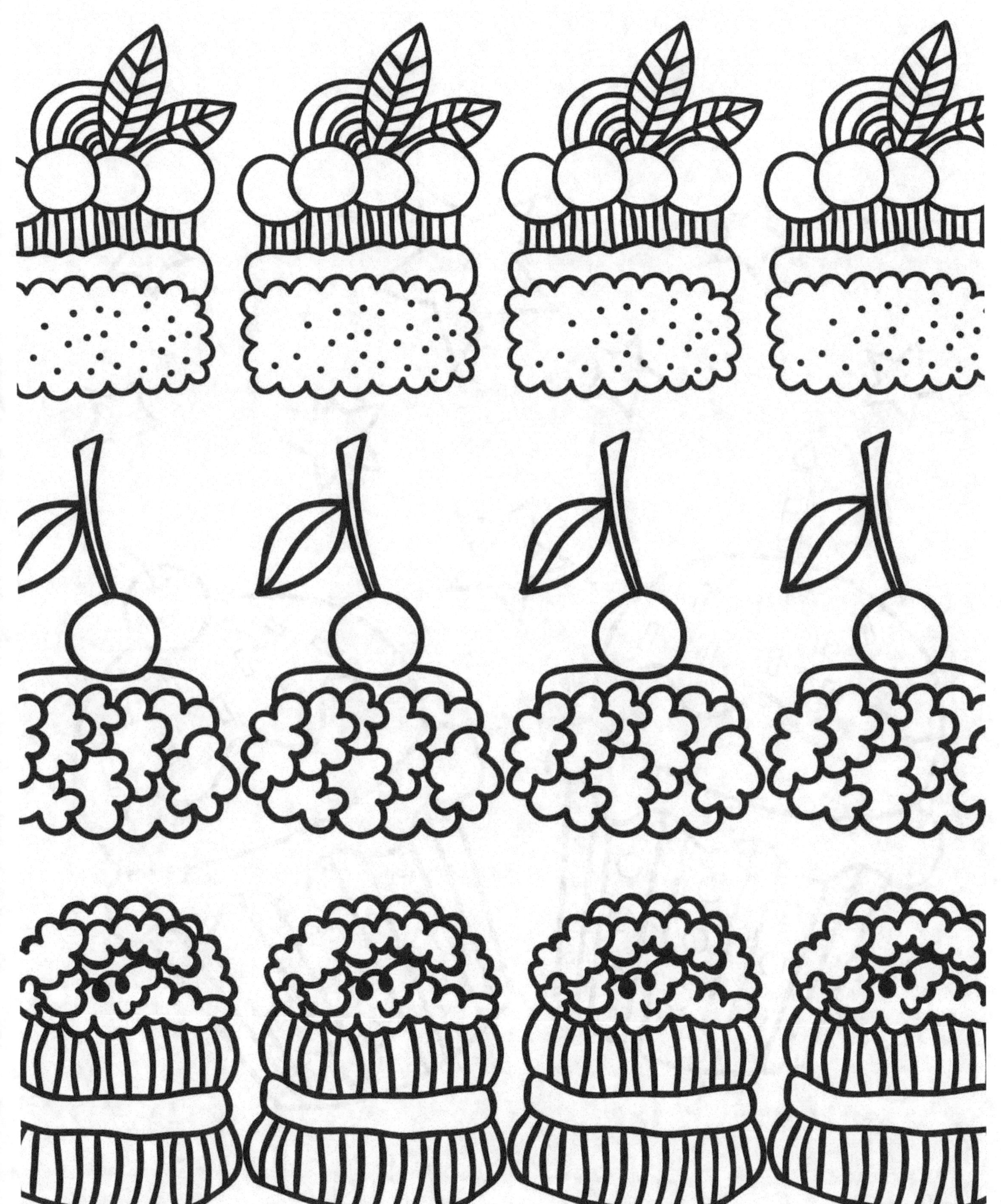

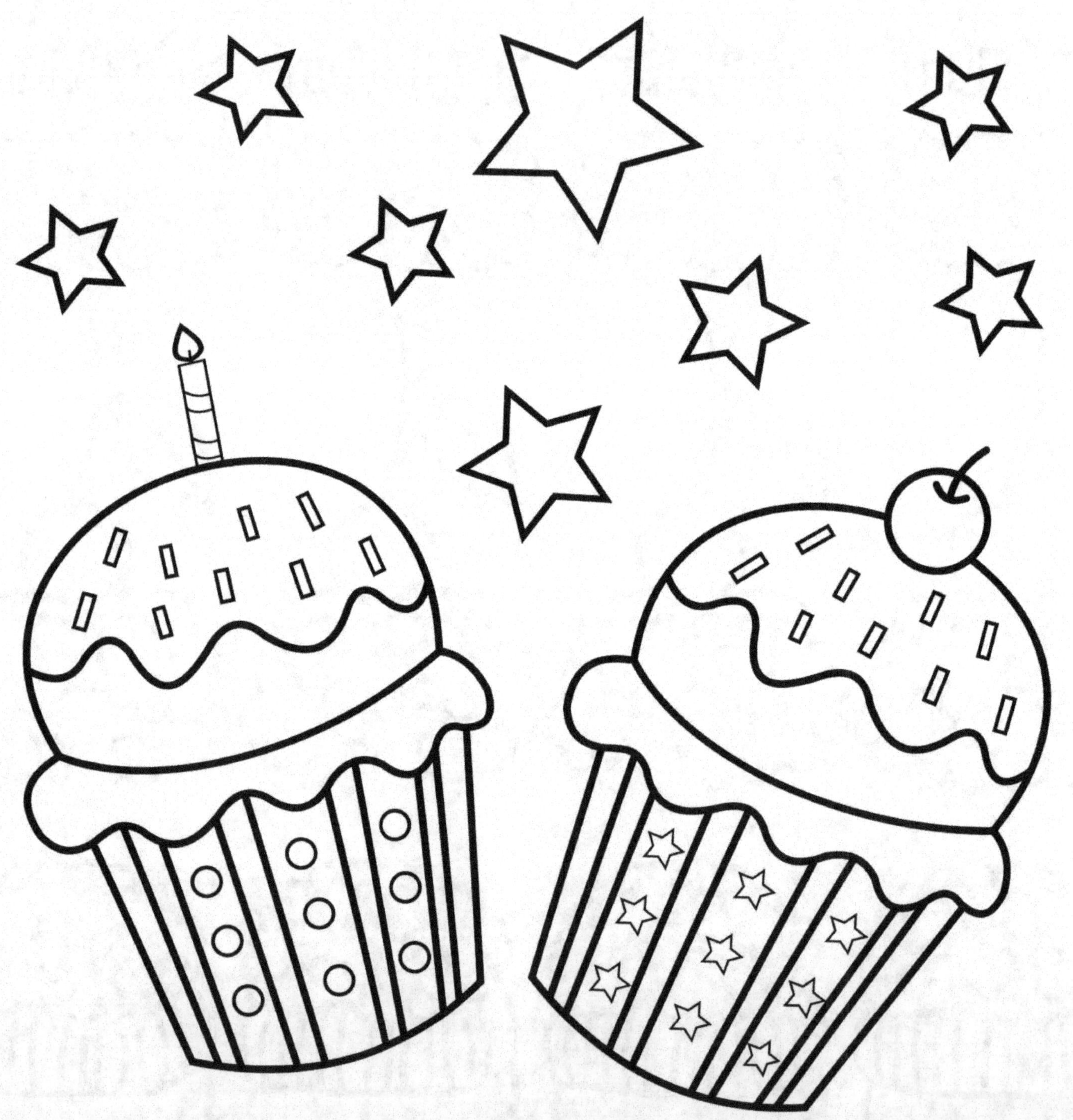

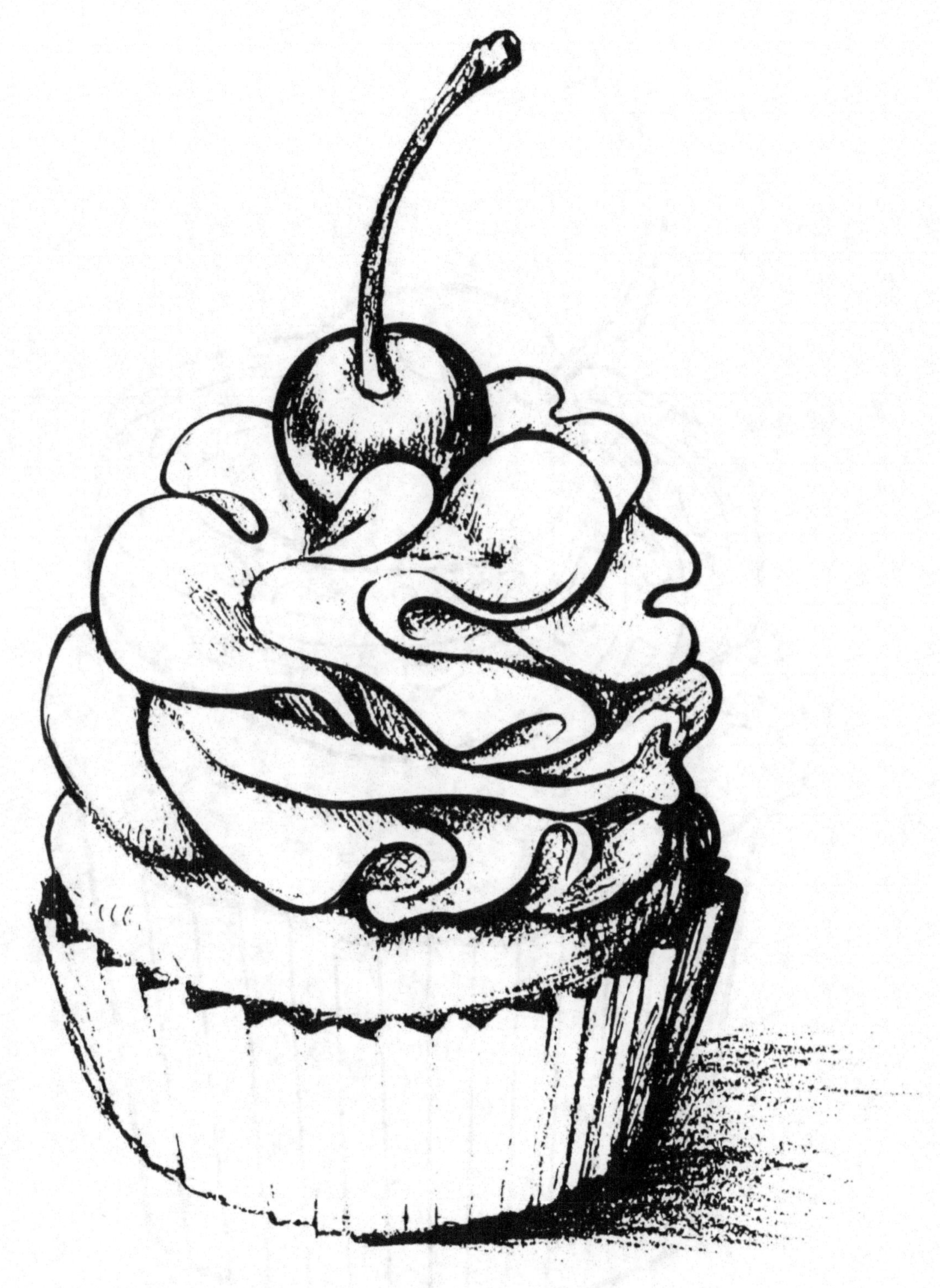

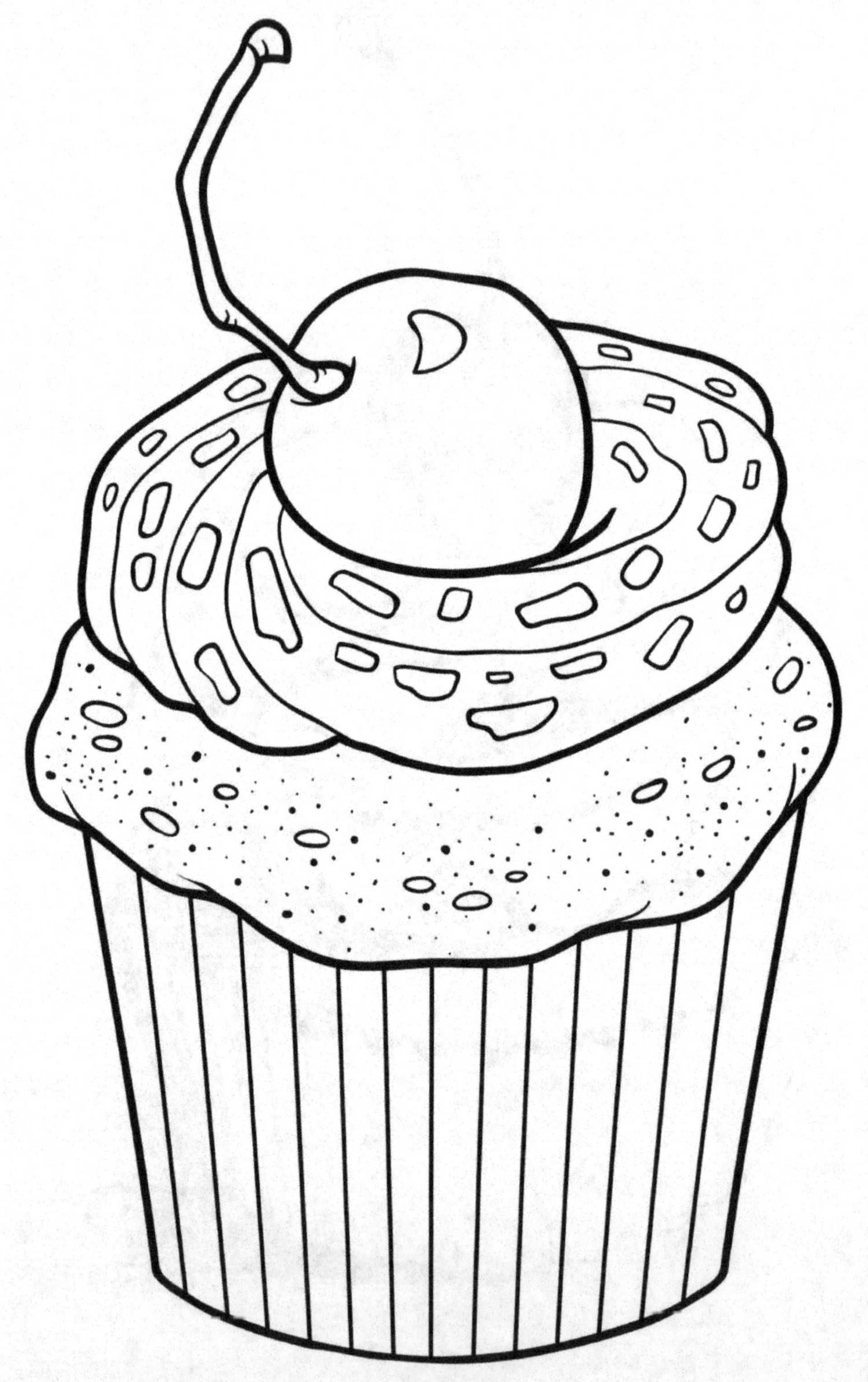

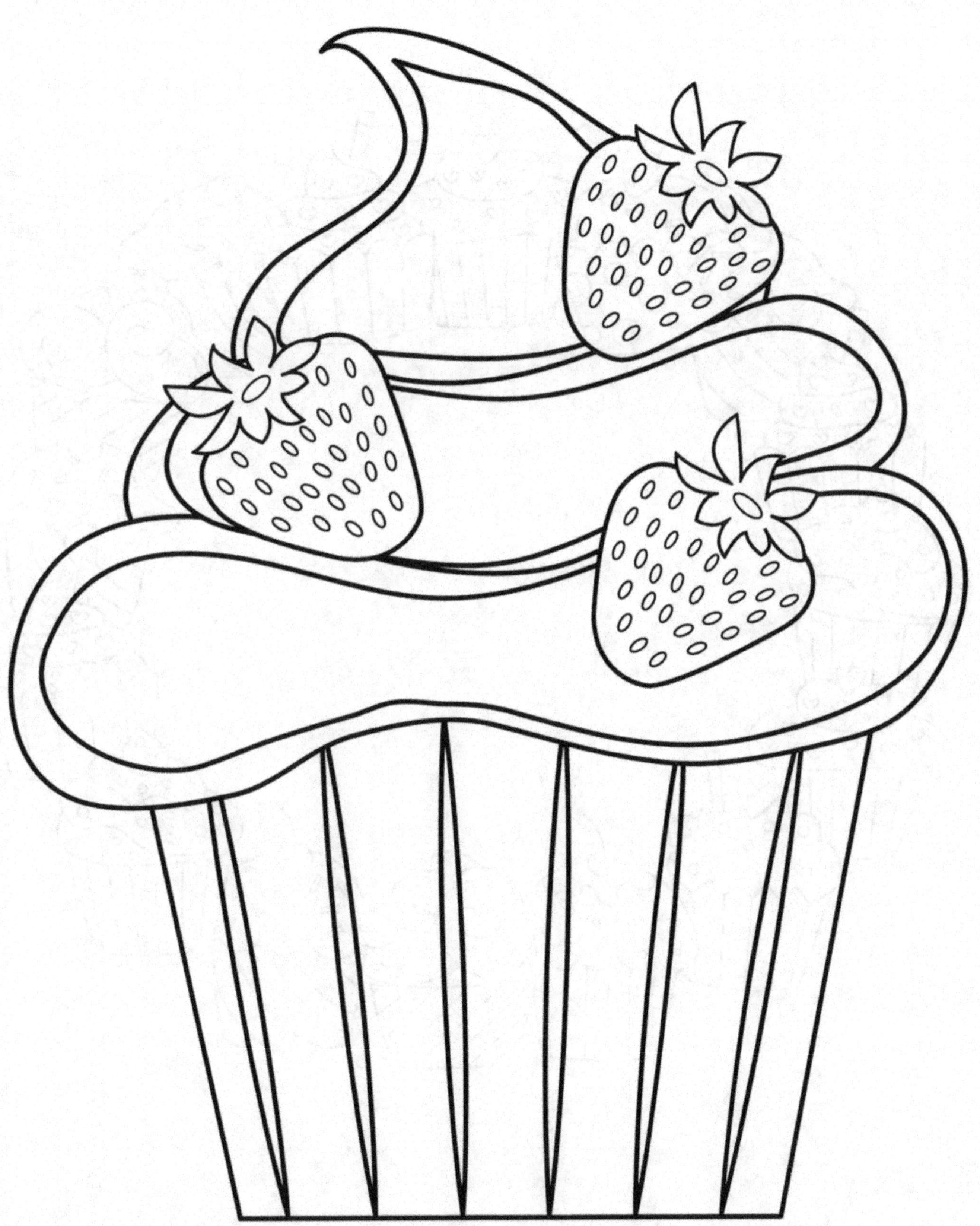

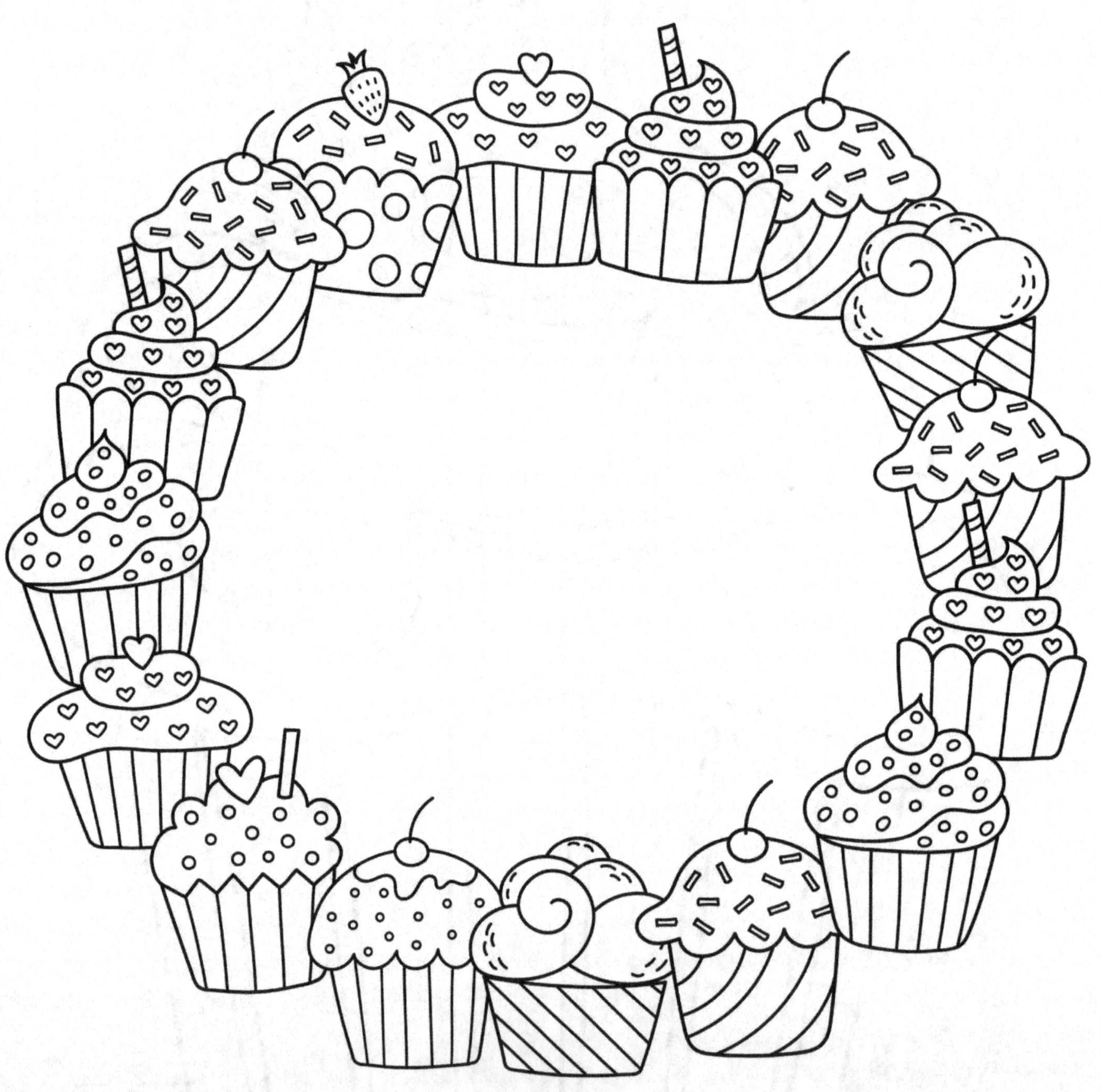

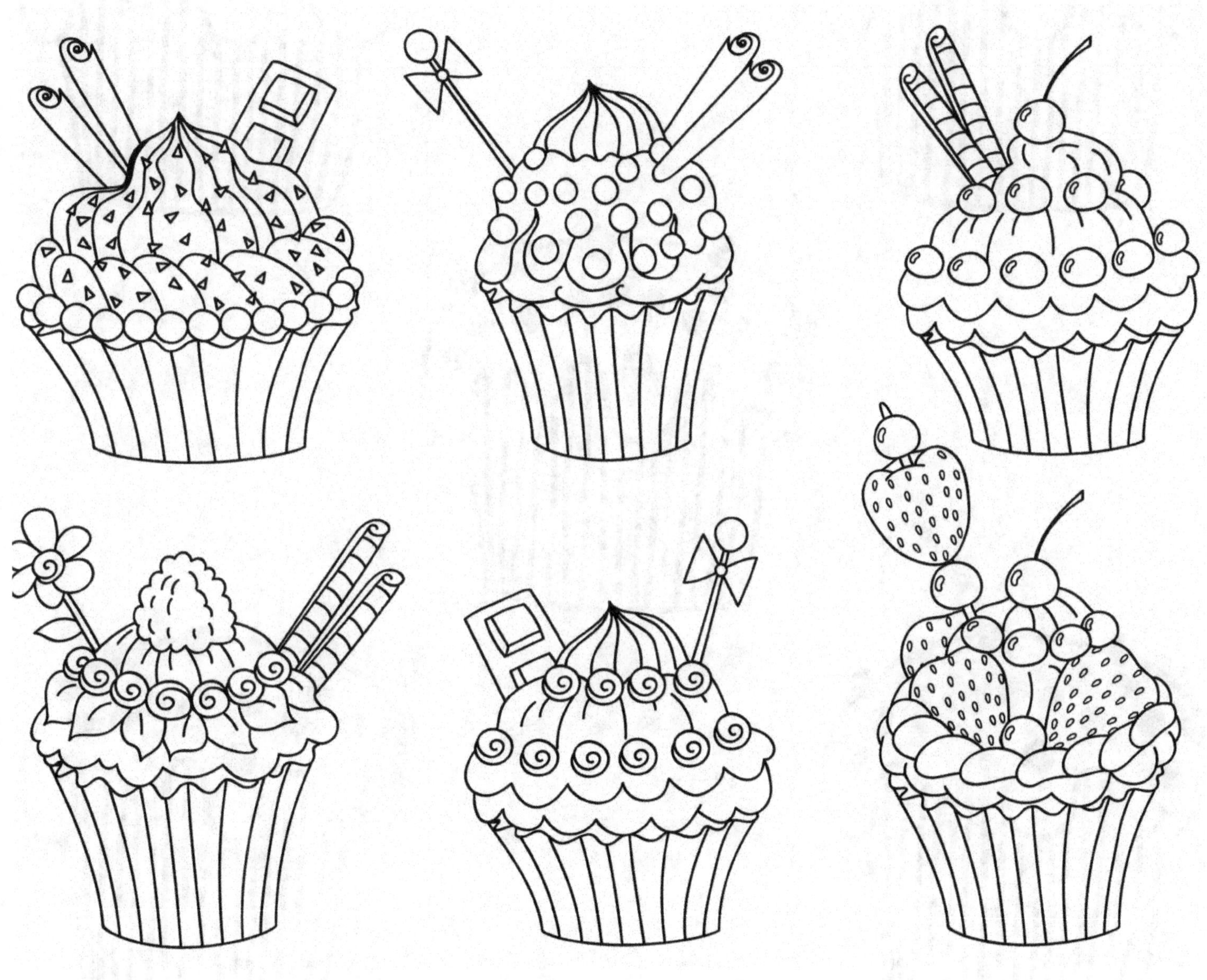

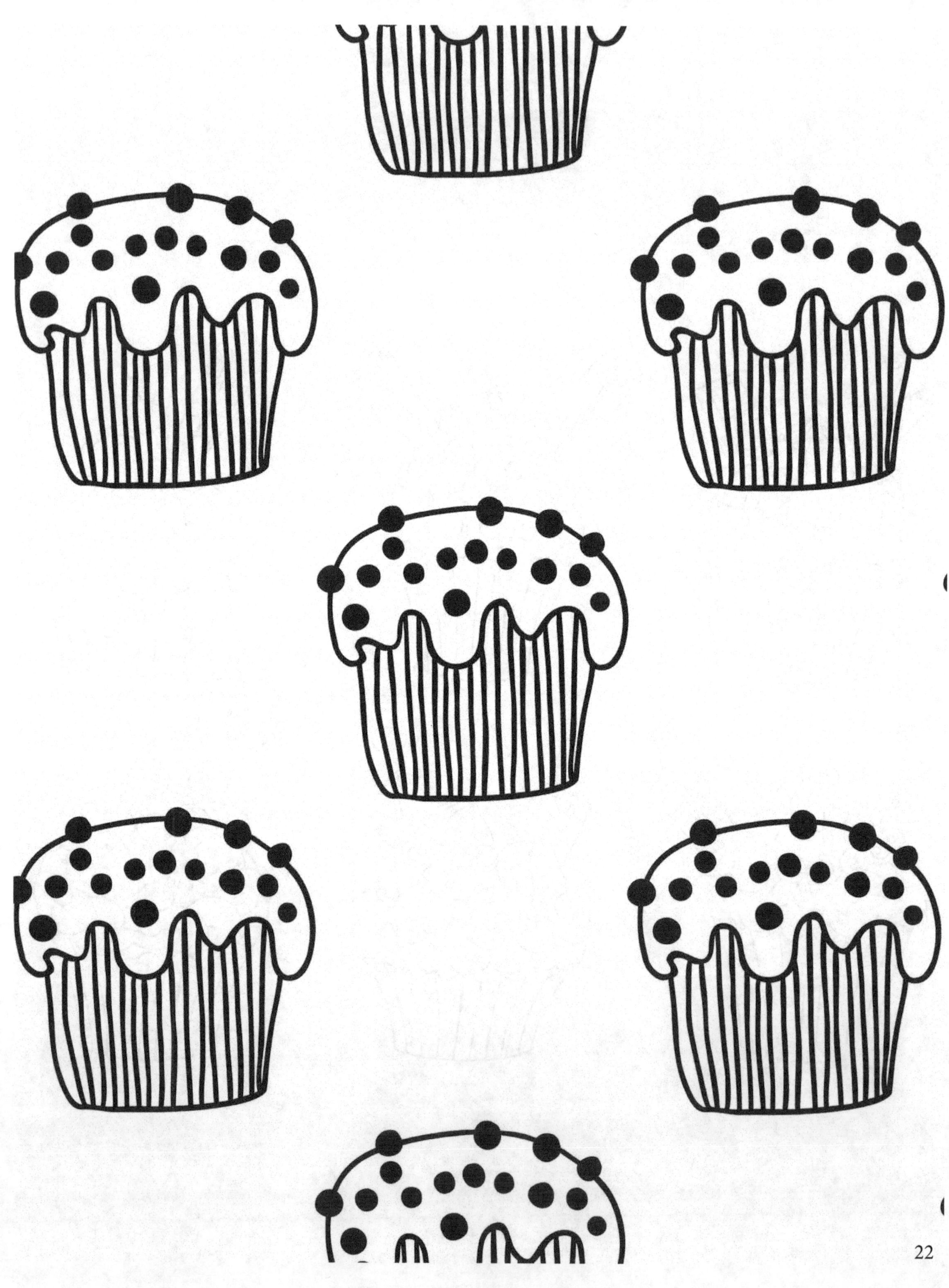

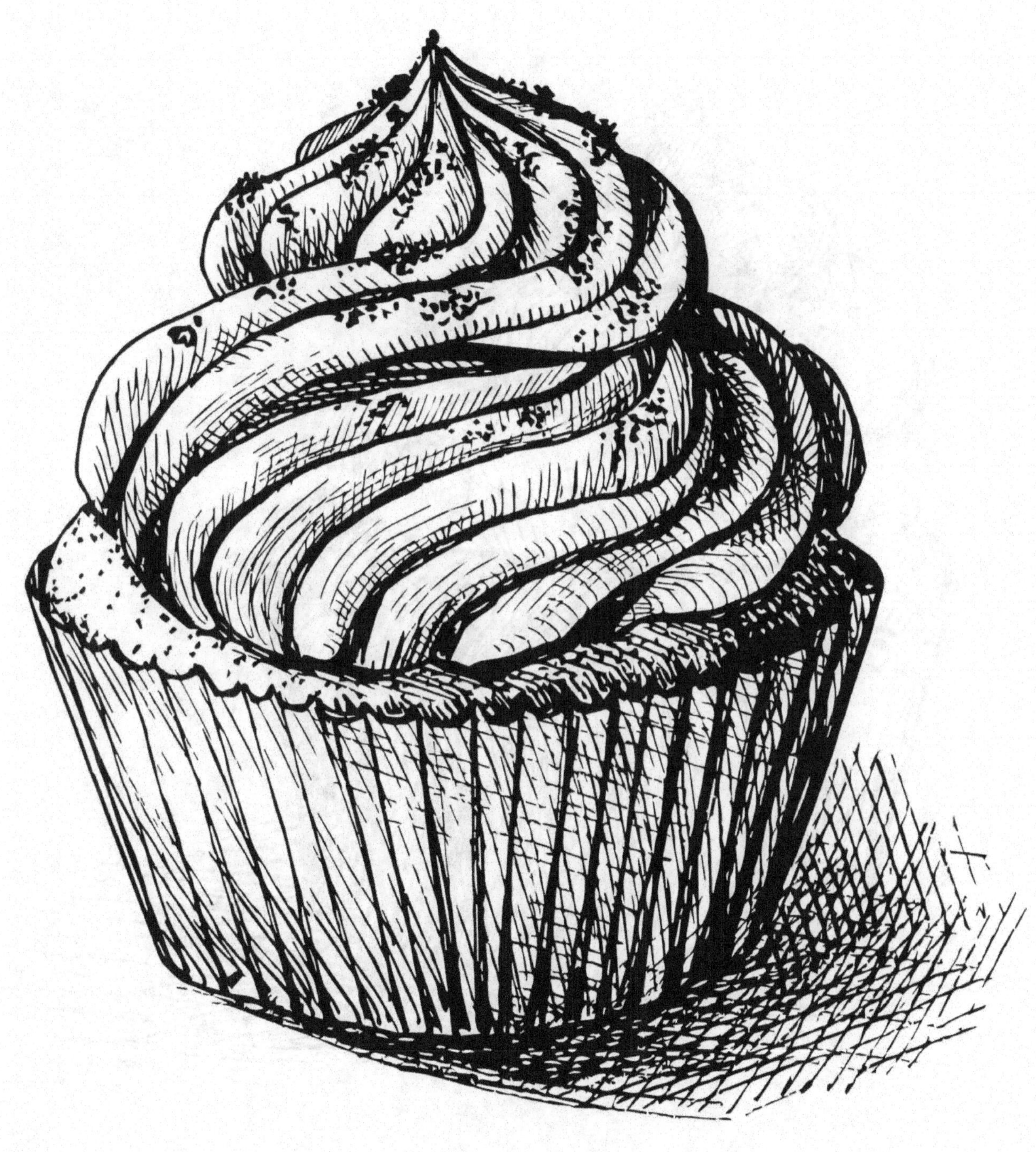

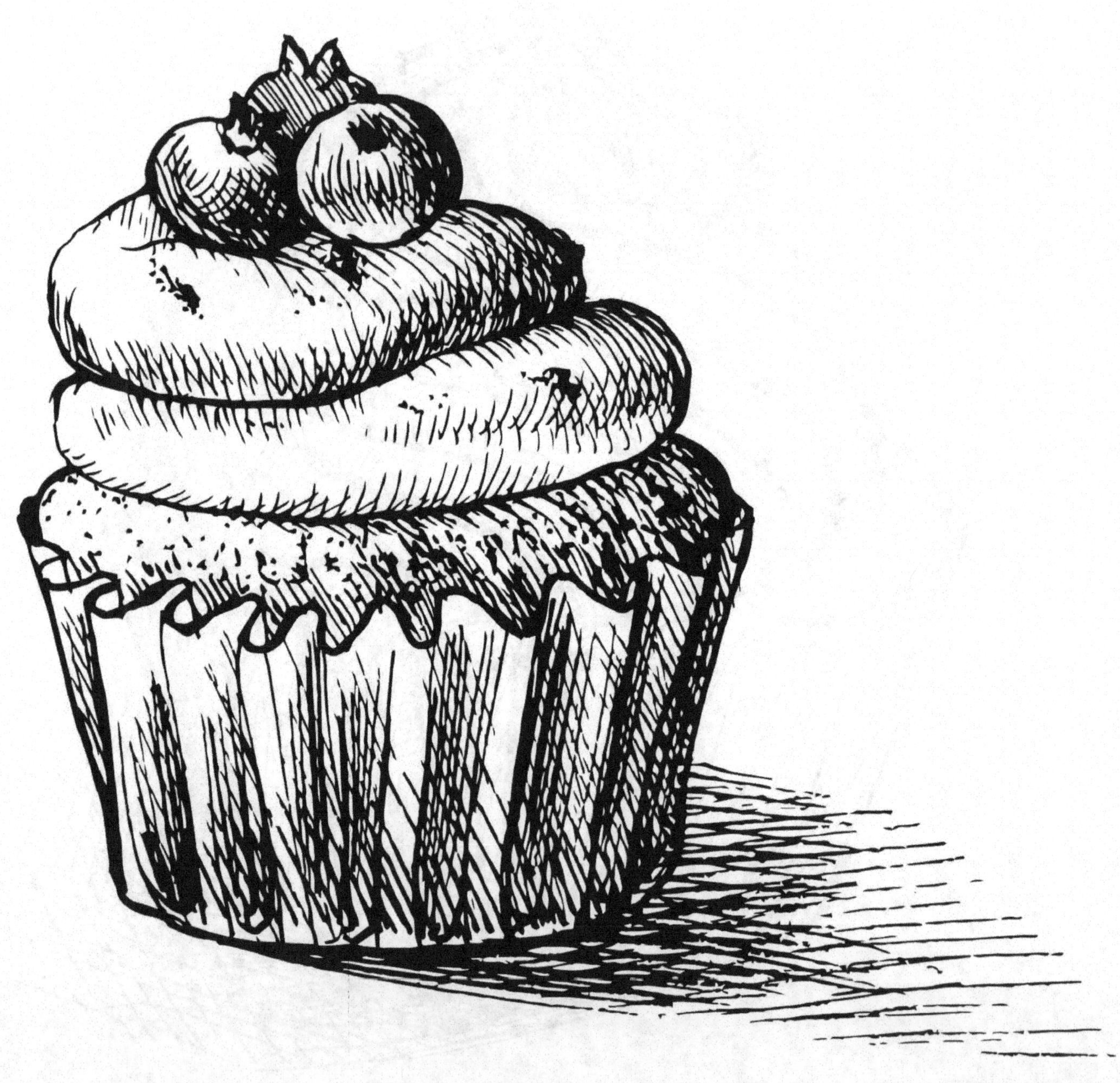

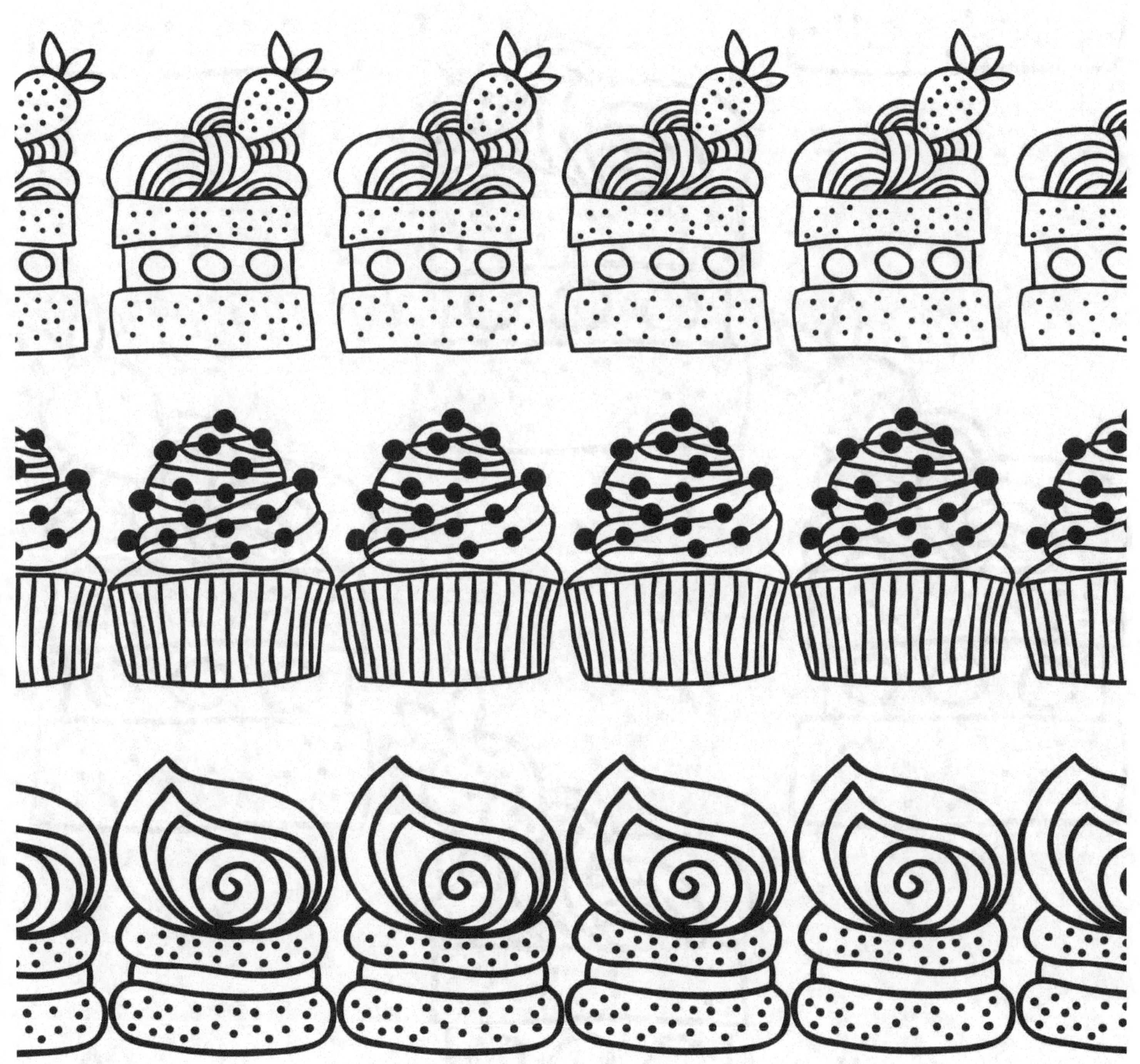

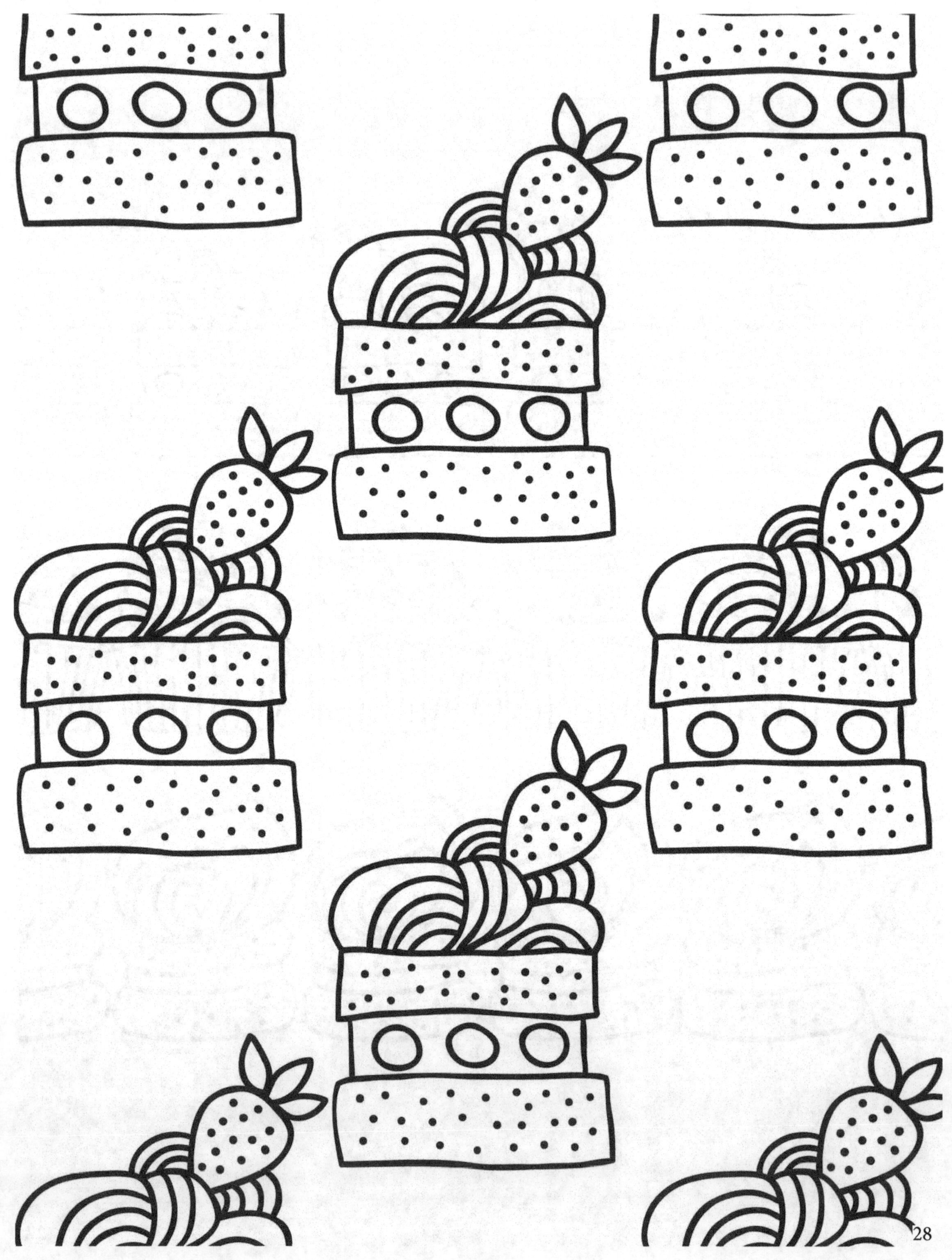